I0841022

AMERICA'S DAFT ERA

by Karen Kellock Ph.D.

Manual for Superior Men

**A complete theory based on Einstein physics,
Political Psychology, Systems Theory
and Archetypal Psychiatry.**

FORMULA

**All success attraction
All disease obstruction
All recovery elimination**

You must fast on all three

OBSTRUCTIONS:

**People
Habit
Food**

AMERICA'S DAFT ERA

I always felt the contradictions and false accusations of liberals. The modern woman wants to "get out more" and sees home as her prison, her husband a bore. Narcissism is emptiness not self-love--the latter is for drawing boundaries not being a snob. Narcissism is not about looking in the mirror but emptiness dependent on approval of others. At the other end is the queen with mile-high walls and extreme vetting of anyone she's meeting.

FOOLS CUT THRU DAFT

EFFECTS OF NARCISSISTIC ABUSE
PRIVACY INVADED: I HATE IT
EMPATHS TARGETED BY NARCS
THE FOOL: MOCKED BUT NEEDED
THE FOOL SPEAKS TRUTH
THE SOCIAL MISFIT IS IT
LEARN ABOUT HIM/FORGET HIM
UNHAPPINESS JUST FROM THINKING
PEOPLE COME IN DIFFERENT SIZES
MEN CONTROL OUR WEIGHT

FOOLS CUT THRU DAFT

EFFECTS OF NARCISSISTIC ABUSE

The effects of narcissistic abuse can last a lifetime but knowledge inoculates you from this guy.

Idealization, sudden rejection, questioning self for a time of long duration: what destruction.

You wanna talk to the narcissist, make him understand. He gives so little it's an addiction.

The emotional ups/downs [to suffer] made life hell on earth til I finally woke up to myself sir.

These types WANT you to suffer and enjoy watching it or causing a stir. Think about that dear.

It's SIMPLE. How to dethrone the narcissist: find your own validation and control your reactions.

If you get ahead he's a jealous monster. You know this in your head so you fear going faster.

Love is a spirit which brings you both together so as it elevates you it elevates him in like manner.

PRIVACY INVADED: I HATE IT

It hurts when privacy is invaded, even by a spouse. Tho' we're one I'm still human and nervous.

The hypersensitive Nancy Raegan said: "it physically HURTS me when suddenly losing privacy."

It's much more profitable to wait for the RIGHT time than to lose faith and grab at straws, aye.

FOOLS CUT THRU DAFT

Stop being triangulated. The minute another girl enters the scene remove yourself quickly.

They saw me as the fool: dull-witted, inarticulate, unable to conform and totally useless too.

There's a big difference between attacking "The Church" vs. local churches thusly cursed.

The false church is everywhere. Paul said it and it's true today: we SHOULD be watchmen & pray.

Churches run by women go pagan or get gross hon'. Like classes on fellatio or "pleasing husband".

The modern church, the pagan runaway heretic church, does what it thinks not by verse.

As soon as social deacons and bossy women run the church they do what society thinks sir.

Men, in contrast, go by the book. Men need to take control and put things right as God spoke.

I've even heard of modern churches jumping on the diversity [DEI] train: unChristian, insane.

For Christians never see people's colors to begin with nor their income. True Christianity is freedom.

EMPATHS

When we don't qualify those we lend ourselves to it's Toxic Empathy: loving others but hurting us.

Empaths pick up on subtle emotional cues the others miss: I've often been hired by the stressed.

The others cannot discern the person is struggling but an empath can feel it immediately.

FOOLS CUT THRU DAFT

THE FOOL

The fool is freer and happier than those burdened by wisdom. He speaks truth with abandon.

The fool lacks wisdom to craft lies or manipulation, he's like a kid as he blasts open visions.

Unencumbered with learning & convention the fool comes to profounder truths as I did son.

The fool calls himself wise but the wise man knows himself to be a fool. Shakespeare

So-called "intellectuals" are usually just purveyors of the current narrative, i.e. they aren't it.

One "intellectual" believes what is false and the other fool refuses to believe what is true.

THE FOOL SPEAKS TRUTH

The fool speaks truth the others dare to utter and this brings instant relief to everyone altogether.

They love the fool cuz people know it has to be said and no one else has the courage or head.

We need the fool's blunt observations to keep our inner lives from being a sterile wasteland.

Fresh ideas and new energy: that's the contribution of the fool but they still don't trust him see.

Those too afraid to challenge the status quo like the fool come against him: that's the rule.

His persecutors would never risk their reputation by being authentic like that foolish lunatic.

FOOLS CUT THRU DAFT

Fools represent values rejected by the group as they oppose social norms especially the cruel.

THE SOCIAL MISFIT IS IT

The fool is seen as an incompetent social misfit ostracized for his deviant rebelliousness.

The irony is every group must have such a figure for they are the agents of change for sure.

Culture becomes lively giving space to figures functioning to uncover prevailing hypocrisy.

Dwarfs, hunchbacks and the deformed had special wisdom, forced to find an inside kingdom.

From humiliation, loneliness and suffering they're forced to rely on inner resources see.

LEARN ABOUT HIM/FORGET HIM

Learning about narcissism pushes him outa your mind since you see he's not a possibility, aye.

He's not safe, he's not sane, he's crazy and inane. He won't fix it just comes back and gives it again.

If family hates you, treat it like Trump cuz the foe hates him too yet he stays happy & shrewd.

They're so into the surface personality when they see red flags they ignore it fearing loss see.

They don't wanna let go of the dream, the grand images in their head so ignore it all instead.

Believing the dream and ignoring the facts, easily swept up into the charisma of cads.

FOOLS CUT THRU DAFT

Don't hold onto what you believe he can be. That's a serious trap for women: open eyes/see.

People miss the mark by looking at fantasy not reality: a nightmare called a dream see.

The lifetime resentments from the men I knew had to be dealt with daily with forgiveness renewed.

Nothing is gained by going back since you can't change the facts so what's the payback?

It's inefficacious to constantly go back and that's why Satan triggers the memory: sad.

UNHAPPINESS JUST FROM THINKING

She-macho is impulsive, reckless, irresponsible, aggressive, lacking guilt, remorse or empathy.

Get rid of all resentments each morning. Get it over with, the most important thing for stress.

Take no offense: that's what the lord instructs. Get it over each morning then enjoy your lunch.

Most unhappiness comes from unnecessary thoughts like sad or tragic memories of pain/loss.

Or we think of nonexistent problems which generate the same brain chemicals as if it's all real.

What a waste: Why not just stay present and everything past or future say "I don't care".

Unnecessary unhappiness comes from unnecessary thoughts which plague us: pray to God.

Here their lives are ruined by unnecessary negative mind activity and they don't know it see.

FOOLS CUT THRU DAFT

PEOPLE COME IN DIFFERENT SIZES

Asian female body is 30 lbs < Western women. They gotta gain weight or people don't like em.

The Asian body proves size is relative. What you call "curvaceous" I have a problem with.

What they call "curvaceous" i see as jiggling thighs, breathlessness and not feeling just right.

When I'm 96 lbs. at 5' 3" I feel amazing with total energy without let up, working hard all day.

MEN CONTROL OUR WEIGHT

At age 16 my boyfriend got mad when I lost weight. That was the first time I felt like a slave.

Am I really supposed to have my body the way someone else wants it? No sir/that's bunk.

Who hates you, all the fat women in your group after you lost all that weight? Yes, that's it ok.

I hate the way clothes fit with pulchritude. And with age it's not elegant like a model dude.

Societies get fatter together. And then they all call the thin "ugly"--it's a relative/social hypnotizer.

First I'm startled but then disappointed. I'm jealous of my privacy making them want more of me. **END END END**

DARKNESS

BOUNDARY BUSTERS
REPENTANCE OF THE PAST
WEAK WOMEN, DIVESE LUSTS
CHRIST WAS BETRAYED
FOOLISH FLATTERY
AVOIDING OLD AGE: SUICIDE
GAMES OF FEMALE NARCISSISTS
THE NARCISSIST PROMISCUOUS
DUNNING-KRUGER EFFECT
DAILY DEEDS UNTO DEATH
FAST ONE DAY A WEEK
FAME AVERSION
CREATIVE COMPLETION

DARKNESS

The first part of life are your lessons and those are hard friends if you didn't listen to parents.

The second part of life is reaping the benefits of having learned your lessons, or loss and death.

The world will teach em lessons their parents couldn't and it'll be hell on earth for those nuts.

What they call normal dating I call female slave conditioning and baby I'm not having any.

Even in this age of malevolent egalitarianism people need exalted exemplars to admire son.

BOUNDARY BUSTERS

You're mad at a past invasion of your boundaries, well why the hell did you let him in honey?

Women are sexually vulnerable and they're smaller so why would you ever let men in dear?

You're sorry for what you did, now let it go. You were caught in a web, pulled down low.

To go thru the muck and mire--learn from your mistakes--you gotta eat some crow I think.

I was misjudged my whole life and gave up defending myself. Like a lamb to slaughter, hell.

They're only interested in you when convenient for them. You know this inside friend, amen.

So you made mistakes. What's left? Utter perfection and thru Jesus the entire past is erased.

DARKNESS

You have every reason to fear man. Don't get involved, don't let em in/don't enter car ma'am.

Most young males are children in adult bodies. Avoid these most unless you like treachery.

REPENTANCE OF THE PAST

Once you've repented and life has totally changed, any mention of the past is a lie and deranged.

A nobody had he not been born into royalty took a wrecking ball to what gave him everything.

His fluff page is full of "hard won wisdom" about how powers that be have made him a victim.

Because women care for infants they must be vigilant about outer threats and taught to resist.

Under slave conditioning they've lost sensitivity to threat and even see strangers as friends.

Liberals have such dirty minds they fill in the gaps of false accusation. The solution: relocation.

In eldering we mine the past for gems. Lucid recall brings greatness, elation and wisdom.

Don't ignite grudges looking back because you were both younger then, it was a SYSTEM.

If you're happy with friends and pets that's as good as it gets and it's positive: that's best.

Eldering is telling the truth and for this the kids will line up at your booth for it relieves them too.

It's not obsolescence or decline but the world calls it inferior tho' traditionally it is most high.

DARKNESS

The old men got the first seat in the senate for they were most respected/never neglected.

Every single traditional culture respected the elders of the tribe but now they're just "gonna die".

WEAK WOMEN, DIVESE LUSTS

But the weak woman stuck in diverse lusts WANTS the man in her house and there it all starts.

Men as pollinators want into her house [the nester] but honey how does this look to the neighbors?

Stop worrying over age and just tell yourself: I'm gonna live to 100 with much more to build/sell.

Living into old age shows you've taken care of yourself with much wisdom to tell. ENJOY it/stay well.

Had I not let men into my house it woulda saved me countless time, sin relapses and money

Above all never let an EX into your house. What does he want, a bootie call? No way doll, the louse.

Elders are peculiar having had more years to get this clear so BE God's peculiar delight ya hear.

The road is rougher if you don't learn it from parents. You may even be killed learning it, heck.

Tell self you deserve abundance, no imposter syndrome. Enjoy the fruits of labor, you've won.

Relax. Success does NOT come from east or west but God who puts ONE up/the other down.

People are pugnacious, angry/woman hating so I beseech you to stay home and avoid dating.

DARKNESS

Plan on being a hundred and if you don't at least you were optimistic in old age/no groans.

CHRIST WAS BETRAYED

Christ was betrayed by those closest so why would we expect anything more from the masses?

When truth-tellers are put in prison you know we're in a new season and it's just beginning.

It was horrible being amongst the low. Like prison without protection from the gross and slow.

You're betraying yourself being around bad associations, a sign your consciousness is broken.

To be dominated by the gross/low is the best possible teacher of a future leader you know.

To be tyrannized by the lowest is all you gotta knowest about the masses to rule best.

Is he a malevolent narcissist or just on meth? Most are in that group and it makes em mad.

FOOLISH FLATTERY

Foolish flattery is as bad as virtue signaling and I'm not having any and neither should you see.

Little did I know the hardest period of my life was just beginning: the season of treason.

The alcoholic is such an expert social manipulator that his wife ends up psychotic I swear sir.

Maturity is: not putting up with things anymore. Boundaries: expanding mentally as you soar.

DARKNESS

Checklist on how to destroy a nation: attack the family, attack men and sexualize children.

Man is a pollinator, he wants sex. If she gives in she's a slut but refusing she wins marriage and love.

The enemy tried to destroy me with everything they've got. The answer: repent [a lot].

"I got no friends cuz they read the papers." That's humans, that's how they are.

She wasn't a slut but a traumatized human being with collapsed morals and boundaries.

He's just as bad as all of em--a high wig in woke companies. He's just as dumb/seeks to please.

As an elder your judge and jury are all gone/dead. Now you're on top: tell youth truth instead.

AVOIDING OLD AGE: SUICIDE

Two friends suicided in their sixties, unwilling to "endure old age"--but it's the crown of glory.

Repeated trauma changes your DNA: you're now hypervigilant forever despite what they say

It didn't damage you forever, stop saying that. It made you better and best: hypervigilant!

We can't stay young forever and we all die, that's the truth guys. But there's an afterlife.

Say: don't worry about it for a week then the relaxation triggers the work without cease.

Once you start you'll never stop I can promise you that so just relax and the trigger is God's.

DARKNESS

The Hero's Path is crooked and thorny but eventually ends in Victory. Have faith in causality.

GAMES OF FEMALE NARCISSISTS

The biggest marker of a female narcissist is total disregard for your boundaries or resistance.

The female narcissist loves to triangulate or pit you against the another in raw hate.

The she witch has old boyfriends around to maintain inappropriate closeness with her exes

She's even triangulated her current partner against an old flame: these are her games.

THE NARCISSIST PROMISCUOUS

Miss Narcissist will even be promiscuous or with other's partners inappropriately intimate.

Artists and actresses must give up salt lest they show bulges and protuberances, I kid you not.

These are women who need multiple sources of approval supply. The phone is their weapon, aye.

Take mixed signals as a "no". They are one foot in, one foot out and that's a NO-GO.

If they only see you when they want something to ever prioritize them is insanity see.

Mixed signals equals NO, remember that. Don't give him another thought the dirty rat.

God said believers would not be condemned. That's gotta mean He erases the past man.

Planning for the future and being on time is also white supremacist so when you see em, resist this.

DARKNESS

DUNNING-KRUGER EFFECT

Dunning-Kruger Effect: Total ignorance combined with confidence they're right/the best.

Democracy: the theory the common people know what they want/deserve to get it, good and hard.

Equity means one thing: certain groups will benefit and certain groups will be attacked see.

We want equality of opportunity not outcome for the latter's impossible lest you force em.

All standards and following rules is "white supremacist" while fluffing off is not they insist.

God's vengeance on my enemies: they were not able or wise enough to leave California see.

Total ignorance and absolute arrogance equals disaster due to the progressive menace.

DAILY DEEDS UNTO DEATH

Will I live longer cuz I don't eat or drop dead like everyone says? I'm up all night while they slept.

I'm the one existing on cat naps, with high energy all day, a workaholic who never ever stops.

It's eating that is the encumbrance, stuffing: a body full of undigested meals and building.

Why do they keep eating? It is emotional hunger, a salve for lost hopes or rejection by dopes.

Skinny with wrinkled extremities indicates a blocked lymph. Fast and one day it all starts to lift.

DARKNESS

It's Einstein: less is more--energy! Don't add [muscles] but subtract for elasticity of a cat.

Bulimics die while in the act. Tell young girls to think of that and it may stop this trend of brats.

Just resign yourself: I'm not eating on the Lord's Day. It's the best day of the week to do it I'd say.

Two days no-salt and begin to see the patchy and itchy skin diminish as hydration is raised.

If she doesn't have the verbal armory to defend her position she's thrown into an ED prison.

De-salt body in 2 days and skin texture is changed: dryness leaves as hydration is raised.

Make sabbath day the highest day of the week: to show your love to the Lord, just don't eat.

FAST ONE DAY A WEEK

Fast one day a week to return to factory settings. It's not a chore but the best day I guarantee.

Take one day to repair all the cumulative damage done in the week. A return to perfection see.

Not just a return but far BETTER than before the bad cycle began. Imagine that Madam.

All I want is butter, flour and sugar. I just want desserts/don't even bother with the other.

The other thing I love is ice cream: so sweet, fatty and satisfying, to my dry throat so cooling.

Ice cream or Scottish shortbread with tea for breakfast and if I get hungry later {rare] a few nuts.

DARKNESS

Ice cream entails little digestion because there's no fiber. Read Fiber Menace to see this bummer.

Just don't eat and the body snaps into shape. This is hard to believe but God made it easy ok.
Women: Men are bigger, DUH! So you don't let em in, you don't get involved so quickly sista'.

FAME AVERSION

I'd get so anxious over fame I'd call 911 thinking I was having a heart attack-- quite insane.

Fame aversion feels like the entire universe and multitudes are pressing on the crown.

The crown is sovereign: it's the True Self once boundaries are laid and there's no invasion.

Fame history is full of basket cases who became famous once they worked out their problems sis.

The best saints WERE the worst sinners. Starting as madmen they became cultural saviors.

I wasn't a bad person, just addicted to alcohol. it's genetic but trauma's at the base of it all.

Suddenly everything reassembles into a simpler, higher, efficient matrix and you go with it.

CREATIVE COMPLETION

You've completed your work, now wait to be discovered. You're a planter, waiter, then harvester.

Divine vindication MUST happen. You'll come to their mind/they'll see what they did man.

Suddenly a new style came thru and that formed the matrix of the next 15 years of all-day writing.

DARKNESS

Suddenly an amorphous vision was locked into place via formula: a simple paradigm for ya'.

Why God chose me as a vessel is all I wanna know. What a privilege from on high: so below.

Simplicity in speech is a rare art, aye. The true genius is terse, laconic and wise.

"I will make a way for you, I'm fighting your battles, prayer is the way, my timing is ALL." God

AMERICA'S DAFT ERA

NARCISSISM ISN'T WHAT YOU THINK
TRAUMA AND MORAL/BOUNDARY COLLAPSE
SEE THE SYSTEM FOR RELIEF
JOLLY JIMMY PHONIES
YOU NEED VISION
STUCK AT HOME NEUROSIS
BUILD STRENGTH TO NOT CAVE IN AGAIN
YOUR MAN'S A PROBLEM SOLVER
ABUSERS TAUGHT TO BE SOCIAL
DON'T GO BACK TO SHOW EM
THE POTTER'S WHEEL IN A SHACK
FATAL ATTRACTIONS
PEOPLE ARE THE ONLY PROBLEM
SEXUALLY DEBASED GRISL ARE MEAN
WE'RE NOT ALL EQUAL
LAYING EVIL SEEDS
IN SOLITUDE THE WORLD LIGHTS UP
ESCAPE MORE NOT LESS
JOY OF FALLING OUTA STRUCTURE
TO KNOW PEOPLE STUDY THE HOLOCAUST
NOW COMPLETE, PRAY
RELATIONSHIPS TAKE SKILL SETS
POST-WAR CYCLES OF LOW KEY
APATHETIC TO DEPTH
DEGRADE TO REMAIN RELEVANT?
COMMUNIST TAKEOVER
BARBARIANS LINED UP AT THE. GATE
MULTI-LEVEL ABUSE
FRUSTRATION LEADS TO AGGRESSION
DUMBED DOWN MILLENNIALS
ONE WORD IS ALL IT TAKES
SIGNS OF GLOBALISM
COMMIE CULTS
75 MILLION BROKENHEARTED AMERICANS
THERE'S A PLAN MAN
HOW DO WE LIVE NOW
CENCORIOUS SNIPPY CULTURE

AMERICA'S DAFT ERA

BUT THE GLOBALISTS BLOCKED US
THEY'D RATHER HAVE OBAMA
INTERLOCKING JEALOUSY SYSTEMS
JUST CUZ IT'S LEGAL DON'T DO IT
INFORMED DISSENT VS. PACK DISSENT
MASCULINITY BAD, AMERICA-HATE GOOD
THUG BACKLASH
FEMALE THUGS IN POLITIX
WE'RE SICK OF BEING BULLIED BY CREEPS
WE'RE AWAKE NOT A CULT
AMERICA HATERS ARE DOMINATING
CHIPS ON SHOULDER GETS ATTENTION
SELL COUNTRY OUT/IMPOVERISH NATION
WORTHLESS APOLOGIES
ONE PORN KING DESTROYED THE FAMILY
INSIPID VACUOUS POLITICAL OPINIONS
ELITES INTO THE OCCULT
THEY JUST LOVE THE ACTION
CREEPY OLD PORNOGRAPHERS
THEY WANT ANGER, VIOLENCE AND CLASH
AFGHANISTAN
BOTCHED BY WRONG ASSUMPTIONS
IT'S CLASSIC GROUPTHINK
CONSTANT ERRORS OF INFERIOR MINDS
LAWLESS ELECTED LEFTISTS
GANGS OF YOUNG MALES
AT TIMES LIKE THIS
SUFFER THEN WRITE
EVIL IS A CONSUMING FIRE
THE DISARMED ARE EASILY MANIPULATED
UNEARNED MORAL. SUPERIORITY
THE NRA ARE NICE RATIONAL MEN
ANTIFA HAS COLLEGES AND MEDIA
BARBARIANS IN OFFICE
ANYTHING TO RETRIEVE POWER—*ANYTHING*
PEOPLE ARE SPLIT AND BLIND
SCIENCE EVOLVES LIKE ALL HERDS DO

AMERICA'S DAFT ERA

ANTI-TATTOO IS TABOO
GUN OWNERS CALLED "TERRORISTS"
APOLOGETIC ARGUMENTATION
SCHOOLED TO THINK AMERICA'S BAD
WE'RE LIBERAL = INTELLECTUAL
OBAMA CUT THE MILITARY
THEY'RE DOWN ON WHITE
ONCE YOU SEE THE ENEMY
HOLLYWOOD CONTROLLED BY CHICOMS
LATE LIBERAL SHOVE DOWNS
THEY LOVE THE DEVIANCE OF HURTING INNOCENCE
MINING DOWNWARD FOR HELL
LIBERALS SWITCH WITH THE WINDS
EVIL STINKS
ACTRESS ADORES A CHILD RAPIST
MOORE MORAL CONSCIENCE
THE GODLY ARE OSTRACIZED
CHI-COM OWNED
JOB OF OLDER WOMEN
SEARED CONSCIENCES GET USED TO SIN
GLOBAL WARMING: THEY'RE ONE OF EM
NOW'S YOUR CHANCE TO RISE
HYPOCRASY HOLLYWOOD
HOLLYWOOD HEX
ONLY CONCERN IS MINORITY DEATHS
TRUMP HATE IS BAROMETER
ALL POINTS OF LIBERALISM ARE EVIL
HALF-TRUTHS AND BLURRED LINES
CYCLES OF MANKIND
DESIRE FOR LIBERTY IS SEXY
FIFTY YEARS OF LIBERAL MINDSET
FEMINIST CALLOUS APATHY
HEALTHYMINDEDNESS
WHAT WROTE THESE BOOKS
THE LAST IS YOUR APEX
KELLOCKIALISMS FALL 2021

AMERICA'S DAFT ERA

Wild mood fluctuations from how people treated me: I practiced not caring then was free.

I felt the contradictions and false accusations of the liberal mind even way back then.

Their decline in usefulness is very subtle since they want you to see them as indispensable.

The modern woman wants to "get out more" and sees HOME as her prison, her husband a bore.

I'll say this: You'd better get interested in politics lest inferior men rule over you. PLATO.

The result of failed leadership and politicization of national security is the "Strategy of Hope".

NARCISSISM ISN'T WHAT YOU THINK

Man is most confused when the only barometer of success is how women respond to him.

Narcissism is emptiness not self-love--the latter is for drawing boundaries not being a snob.

The narcissist hates your boundaries, the self-lover understands them completely sweetie.

Self-love is not looking in the mirror but knowing who you are, standing for values, being sure.

Narcissism is not about looking in the mirror but emptiness dependent on approval of others.

AMERICA'S DAFT ERA

Self-love is not narcissism. Self-love is boundaries and narcissists will have none of them.

As a theoretician I tease apart differences and resolve contradictions, that's not arguing son.

In sum you don't know what you're talking about and are winging the whole thing, a faker in sin.

I met a beautiful clean-shaven man and he smelled so sweet--is this just a Western thing?

As an unrepentant sinner all can tell from your demeanor but not your fans those losers.

The narc cares only about winning/having the last word so let em think it as you remove this curse.

Many will seek credit for your success but few or none will accept responsibility for failure sis.

Goodness has nothing to do with it. Don't call me good, only God is good. Jesus Christ

TRAUMA AND MORAL/BOUNDARY COLLAPSE

With trauma there's moral collapse and for years the victim will anguish over: why'd I do that?"

With trauma there's a boundary collapse and for years she'll anguish: why'd I EVER let him in?

How in HELL did she end up surrounded by such bad characters? It's a boundary collapse sir.

Why in HELL did he say such things in public? It was moral collapse, foundation of a lunatic.

At the other end is the queen with mile-high walls and extreme vetting of anyone she's meeting.

AMERICA'S DAFT ERA

The truth is, I'm scared of your sorry self. I sense something and it's not good, it's dark.

The truth is, I sense you'll turn on a dime or you need to be admired by more women with time.

Don't drill down in previous eras too much. Bored or restless we tend to resurrect old grudges.

Previous eras: you were both younger then. Looking back with new eyes you feel victimized.

SEE THE SYSTEM FOR RELIEF

It was a SYSTEM: your immaturities and weaknesses evoked the reactions you're angry about.

That grifter loser took over the house cuz YOU were a weak, needy woman called "hospitable".

The hospitable to the wicked man is despicable--think of the children adapting to his crap girl.

The hospitable to the wicked man is despicable--think of the kids having to take his crap girl.

You cannot correct or recreate the original hug from a loving mother by falling in love over & over.

It's a dangerous world when America's a harmless enemy/treacherous friend: the end.

Liberals never see the danger they'll even minimize slaughter. Separate, dig in, sequester!

Look UP when you need hope in the midst of hopelessness/a miracle in the midst of chaos.

You are relying on the Taliban and you are retreating. That's only ONE message: weakness.

AMERICA'S DAFT ERA

The philistines tend to stuff their homes with furniture to show how social they are: weird.

The artistic want SPACE in their homes with minimal furniture--they like seeing the floors.

I can't stand to stay around the profane for one minute more lest I go insane and feel that pain.

For they are absolutely cruel in their negligence and ego-driven perception for status.

They are absolutely callous in their minimization of danger or adoration of the stranger.

They'll put a hatchet murderer in your house saying he's cool and mean it too, just a lost liberal.

JOLLY JIMMY PHONIES

Liberal false & social: Jolly Jimmy loves everybody but his wife he seeks to torture for eternity.

Many meet the love of their life and hire a therapist to get over the evil soul tie--to love, bye bye.

Once the work is complete just get yourself ready cuz suddenly the spotlight's on you lady.

Tho' I love you I must hire a therapist to get rid of this soul tie/trauma attachment bond: lol.

Unless a buzzcut women must wear hats in the kitchen lest we find hair in food--how sickening.

We went to war to prevent strongholds of terrorism but now it's FAR worse, imminent doom.

As the splintered fragments of self reconfigure into perfection you're the eagle, God's Election.

AMERICA'S DAFT ERA

Living in times like this we ask God: what's my destiny in this confusion, to be a lightning rod?

It's God's Election, it's not you ma'am. We're made in His image and it shows after repentance.

Moral insanity is saying things you can't believe you said and doing things absurd or mean instead.

You've totally lost self-control tho' you be extolled. Self-control is a FRUIT of the spirit/gold.

In my teens and twenties I was totally promiscuous and didn't even realize it. Oprah Winfrey

YOU NEED VISION

You don't need eyes to see, you need vision cuz with ideology you've distorted perception.

Wanting to be liked you'll compromise on everything and achieve nothing. Margaret Thatcher

I was born to do two-liners at my highest point. It took repentance, boundaries, God's anoint.

Salvador Dali didn't care if he was poor cuz if you're famous you're rich and if rich more famous.

Luck is the residue of design and chance favors a prepared mind. It's about FOUNDATION.

The man must "talk" to them and be "emotionally available"--characteristics of females.

What is more important, that he "talk" and be emotional or truly love her by fixing the toaster?

If he behaves more like women then he's a good husband but she loses respect soon.

AMERICA'S DAFT ERA

She complains about his lack of housework but forgets him spending a week replacing the floor.

He's battling long hours of work and and driving and she complains about him not doing the dusting.

He pays the bills. That should be her main thrill but she wants more and more and bitches still.

Be alone for awhile. See what it's like to be unprotected/unprovided for--now just be nice.

Marriage is teamwork and happiness but via the cultural narrative discontent is encouraged.

STUCK AT HOME NEUROSIS

Feminism created the "stuck at home" neurosis when to me it's the best thing about marriage sis.

I wanna be stuck at home dusting and sweeping waiting for your arrival and for that I'm dreaming.

To slow cook a pot roast all day smelling it waiting for your appreciation, that's home isn't it.

I'm stuck in a lovely home and you're not so we'll discuss daily events with cocktail or pot.

Women pressure me to leave home for this and that seeing me as Victorian staying in the pad.

Home wouldn't be a burden & bore if she'd bring impeccable order and create another world.

Once having made your environment reflect your personality you'll NEVER wanna leave honey.

Cuz your home is your protection from a crazy world, a loving fortress where dreams unfurl.

AMERICA'S DAFT ERA

I rarely leave home/can't wait to get back cuz nothing out there's as interesting: that's a fact.

I just wanna look out my window and contemplate in a world of hellish confusion that agitates.

Women: appreciate your husband, the male gender and if you can stay home feel blessed, hear?

BUILD STRENGTH TO NOT CAVE IN AGAIN

Beyond having a loving home and husband, build strength to stand when "out there" again.

Being in the work force five-ten years loses it's luster cuz all we want is home, family, love.

She should have said "why didn't I spend more time working in relationship" not "at the office".

Deathbed insight: relationships are most important, but she wants to throw that out in a minute?

They see childcare as the greatest thing--free of the burden of parenting--but that's false see.

She's "miserable" so she puts the kids in childcare since husband won't do his "fare share".

She's miserable, kids are miserable and he's miserable since he's doing the housework for girls.

Because she hasn't been taught that men are different from her, her expectations end in failure.

Now it's not enough that he dust, he must SEE he needs to dust, he must WANT to adjust.

A widow would love to hear those ballgames again and dust around him, think of that women.

AMERICA'S DAFT ERA

She complains he can't multitask but can't see the extreme **FOCUS** because of that he has.

He can't multi-task but can **FOCUS** so much he solves all problems eventually: the go-to dad.

You provide for me and protect me and I'll do **ALL** the housework and delicious meals too baby.

Me understanding the male brain changed everything and gave me something to work with ok.

YOUR MAN'S A PROBLEM SOLVER

He's the **PROBLEM SOLVER** and if he loves your home he'll do anything til the problems are gone.

Even maga-hat wearers as young as 8 complain of the liberal fascism on campuses, it's insane.

Conservatism is a **RENEWED** movement of true bravery so stand tall and speak of America proudly.

Some older warriors are afraid of the violence but don't listen to us, we've maladapted too much.

BRAVERY by definition: though you stand to lose something you stand up anyway son.

Biden wants you to forget: just slip into the warm bath of civilizational decay come what may.

He has no contingency plans, Biden has one **ACTUAL** plan: they're on their own so forget it man.

Liberals are a herd mentality so if you don't think like them they **ATTACK**– that's the loving man.

I didn't wanna let em in, I was bored being social so they **ATTACKED** me cuz that's all they know.

AMERICA'S DAFT ERA

If you step outa their herd think they attack like vicious animals. Even old ladies bark ya know.

If you are different they just hate you so will hound you and make others feel that way too.

To self-justify their prejudice they will move mountains to force agreement since the social is it.

Speak your truth cuz who are they in the long run anyway? Haters. David Leatherwood

Speak truth despite their abuse--that's being brave and courageous. Break thru it, stand up to it.

ABUSERS TAUGHT TO BE SOCIAL

Taught to be social, they abused me when I didn't want to. It was an insult my need for solitude.

Millions feel like you but fear speaking out. By you doing it they're inspired to enlightenment.

People are just archetypes and memories just magnetisms of the moment/changing.

In vetting people think of how they've treated you in the past [like in a lower caste]--that's obvious.

Young love is about passion, old love accommodation--we just wanna get thru this day man.

Don't show off when big, just recall how they treated you when small, that's the thing.

Think of how the hoity-toity treated you back then though they were the beloved deacons.

Conservatives have been treated badly for decades so it's hard to think ahead as the ACE.

AMERICA'S DAFT ERA

The people putting you down have nothing going on so create your new reality as royally crowned.

I know you wanna kill em but that's the test all thru history for the knightin': gotta forgive em.

DON'T GO BACK TO SHOW EM

You don't have to go back to show em, they can't even remember their mocking rejection.

It's important they see it so God will lay out your banquet and show em so they believe it.

Joe Biden will be judged by how many Americans were abandoned not by how many got out man.

Who could trust America again, she not only abandons you but hands you over to your enemy?

You can get into crying jags just cuza who you are around. It's a spirit & effects are profound.

Eldering is looking back and seeing the life pattern--that couldn't have been any other way man.

He doesn't care if it's your house, he'll still take control. People don't think like you do you know.

THE POTTER'S WHEEL IN A SHACK

On the Potter's Wheel for 30 years in the desert wilderness and when done, happiness.

On the Potter's Wheel living in a shack on 1000 acres with just a bike and loving every minute.

Elation and exhilaration in the wilderness until "they" came and I felt miserable and lost.

AMERICA'S DAFT ERA

No one knows who's saved or damned. But our interest in this probably indicates we're ok man.

Memory detox is like an onion, unpeeling to the core. I'm now at sixteen saying "Oh My Lord!"

I had long periods of solitude in the desert but when "they" arrived it took months to revive.

After being alone for long periods people felt like a tidal wave of confused energy, an INVASION.

Especially being used to a small cabin or trailer, when "they" arrive it's offensive/get out sir.

A man steps too much in your house and you HATE him and the bible says it–God knows us man.

FATAL ATTRACTIONS

The fatal attraction between the trauma-bonded female and narcissist easily-bored male is LETHAL.

90-90 Rule: 90% of time they're lying, 90% of the others are believing, I'd give up on ALL of em, amen.

Like a moth to the flame she runs back to him again after which he loses interest as predicted man.

Forget your losses disciples because everything comes back to the saints after repentance, doubled.

They're fully engaged as long as you're investing in them but when it calls for the reverse they're gone.

Why'd they go away? They discerned it's becoming increasingly difficult to manipulate you ok.

How did he discern you're getting hep? You question too much, to a narcissist his plans are disrupted.

AMERICA'S DAFT ERA

Queen's ask questions that only kings can answer. Anyone lower reveals his dark motives sir.

Asking too many questions triggers him thinking you're becoming too difficult to manipulate honey.

A narcissist will not hang around someone who's not easily manipulated so try to act like that.

PEOPLE ARE THE ONLY PROBLEM

The only problem has always been people. Alone my universe explodes to a phantasmagoria too.

Guess I should thank a gang of ruffians for changing my personality for good on a higher plane too.

Boys were bad but the girls were worse. They'd search in drawers, gossip, start trouble, curse.

With no ethics/civics taught in schools it's a moral debasement of young males across the world.

Young males are taking over small towns and the cops stand down. It happened in '86 to now.

In closing their eyes to it single mothers allowed more rot to grow and fester, it's their bloody fault sir.

The girls are really shady since they're sexually debased early and it spells doom for society honey.

SEXUALLY DEBASED GRISL ARE MEAN

These sexually debased young girls are MEAN. Is there wrath amongst you? Then there is SIN.

I've lost my skill set in adapting to downputting males. It was always a mal-adaptation/my health failed.

WE'RE NOT ALL EQUAL

AMERICA'S DAFT ERA

You didn't appreciate me, discarded/went on to another like we're all equal--what a silly fellow.

Boys are violent but girls are insidiously underhanded and shrewd when it comes to calumny/gossip.

I grew afraid of Cindy cuza her adeptitude in managing the grapevine--oh dangerous enemy of mine.

They destroy the reputation of ex-husbands using buzz words they know galvanize the liberal army.

She had me under her total control purely out of fear who she'd tell--just like junior high a social hell.

Tho' he put me thru hell for twenty years, viewed from the outside I was the savage driving him to tears.

My reactions to left brained insanity was [OE] Over-excitability, leading to high con eventually.

With God the outcome is always good and the past will always break down vaporizing to zilch.

I'm sorry I can't compete with your narcissism [total focus on self] cuz for relationship you lack skill set.

You have your fan base, your adoring peanut gallery, enjoy that--but that's not a relationship skill set.

LAYING EVIL SEEDS

Everywhere I went they laid evil seeds against me so they'd hate me like a Jew in Nazi Germany.

Stuck in lower urges and social approvals or a genius going higher preceded by mass upheaval?

Mass upheaval--disintegration--went on for years but this anarchy was fertile/outcome was new.

AMERICA'S DAFT ERA

I got grounded with self-knowledge that I was only happy when alone, a major insight full-blown.

IN SOLITUDE THE WORLD LIGHTS UP

INSIGHT: when alone the whole world lit up, even in a tiny dusty shack in the desert wilderness? Yup

If I could be so happy in a tiny dusty shack **IF ALONE**, that laid out my whole future and plans for home.

But when with people I'd get irritable, irascible, couldn't wait for em to get the hell out, unstable.

I had the genes and the talents but it was the [OE] over-excitability that shot me up like a rocket.

Overexcitability at being imposed on, bored or pressured burst me open to **SOLITUDE** as my only identity.

If unhappy only I had to create the conditions where I always am happy: solitude/high boundaries.

Existence itself generates so much tension and anxiety that's the fuel integrating higher levels.

It's disintegration that propels us so we should welcome crises for growth/persevere to the goal.

Seeing disintegration as a good thing is a relatively new thing and very relieving, just keep believing.

To become an adult with mature dimensions you must first disintegrate from appetites/relations.

ESCAPE MORE NOT LESS

I say get **MORE** into solitude but the world says "take a course on how to be social and love it".

AMERICA'S DAFT ERA

I don't fight against my natural tendencies. I can't forget when refusing how they would confront me.

In the 80's they'd confront me for being antisocial like I was a religious heretic, it just didn't pass go.

JOY OF FALLING OUTA STRUCTURE

The greatest thing about retirement is falling out of structure--like putting on cozy pajamas sir.

Computer era relieved us of social expectations so that was a flowering into creative predestination.

Pot-lucks & barbecues don't get us to heaven it's doctrine but they're reversed: be social, you're in.

Money, fatty foods and prostitutes made him old overnight. It was rather shocking, a blight.

As Biden starts Obama's 3rd term he helps GOP to reorganize into an anti-communist rod of power.

So overexcitable they wanted to lock me up--but when I got alone that welled up energy burst out.

They put 100 in a boxcar with just a pail then left em to die on the tracks as military prevailed: evil.

Why say you'll be celibate now--you mean you weren't before? Why say these things you whore.

Survivors of concentration camps learned to never trust human nature again, that's history's lesson.

If you didn't obey you'd be whipped or killed maybe hung so their faces were scared/hell-stricken.

TO KNOW PEOPLE STUDY THE HOLOCAUST

AMERICA'S DAFT ERA

Why study the Holocaust 75 years ago? It shows where humans go high or low, it's about morals.

Study the Holocaust and you'll never be complacent again. No more brazen brashness or sin.

Quit soul-stabbing with memories of when the devil was in you. God removed the stain, you're cool.

NOW COMPLETE, PRAY

Now being complete, pray you'll come to mind of the God-chosen link while staying in the pink.

War could happen here, don't be complacent. You could be arrested/hauled off for good, stay humble.

Just cuz I was smart and did well in school didn't mean I wasn't attachment/trauma-bonded as hell.

When as a genius/saint you feel people siding against you think of the Holocaust/how it happens fast.

There's a list of things you could do to Jews and get away with it, a double standard of punishment.

They idolized then stepped too far into relational plans then backed out suddenly, no changing that.

They didn't have the skill set to have a relationship so backed out suddenly-- they couldn't do it.

They jumped into a relationship but couldn't sustain it [no skill set] and this understanding explains it.

They were intrigued, couldn't sustain it--but partnership is about consistency, face this.

RELATIONSHIPS TAKE SKILL SETS

AMERICA'S DAFT ERA

They couldn't do it and there's nothing you can do to fix that. It's inside them, a relieving thought.

They could do the first phase [crazy love] but couldn't sustain it [no skill set] so escaped it.

I don't care if it sells I just wanna make a mark. A serious new dent in whatever lights a creative spark.

You can't get it back to where it was in beginning. That's gone, he's moved on, put focus on self hon'.

Anyone can fall in love but it takes skill to maintain consistency in a relationship with adults.

Forget that he was crazy/solicitously in love at first, he withdrew and things never return ya hear?

POST-WAR CYCLES OF LOW KEY

After seeing the depths of evil in WWII people were low-key in 50's then became brazen, arrogantly.

You say I did nothing in those dry years, I say I was doing everything in a fertile anarchy facing fears.

He was crazy in love at first but narcissists are whatever affects them and feelings change fast.

Socialization happens thru peer pressure so the OE overexcites us to break thru/go higher.

To socially adapt—a must—we are constantly picking up radar on repetition, structures to assist us.

Narcissists often have buyer's remorse. They work so hard to get a person then discard em fast.

They got what they wanted, they conquered it. It seemed ideal to them but now inferior/they discard it.

AMERICA'S DAFT ERA

You're easily used cuz that kept him amused but try to move out from under, he's bored/angry too.

They are ever excited by new supply, the chase, a new partner in any case. Easily bored = narcissist.

Narcissists ruled by magical thinking/idealization, meaning problems are solved by the right person.

You no longer seem ideal/solve problems so they get bored like a child with toy--you're out man.

Narcissists get bored with relationships especially when requiring time or energy investment.

He can do first phase, no problem. Crazy love chemicals even sex--but CONSISTENCY will be lackin'

APATHETIC TO DEPTH

A narcissist doesn't give a dam about your "depth" in fact they can't get that close/admit they're lost.

He's totally apathetic to your depth, get that thru your head. Keep it to yourself, write, find friends.

You're not gonna get a deep conversation outa him so stop trying. Face it, he's superficial/charming.

What is seducing you? That charm has seduced many women but it doesn't last, he'll be vacillatin'

How long before you encounter his mean streak? Will he leave you out in the streets like a sick freak?

Man has TWO sides: two nervous systems/brains. The seemingly sweetest got a tiger inside him.

You gotta go VERY slow and easy in the dating phase. Don't get swept up like many others ok?

AMERICA'S DAFT ERA

DEGRADE TO REMAIN RELEVANT?

Don't "long to remain relevant". Just be yourself and don't give a dam what others want = that's grit.

Since they were apathetic to depth you've been stuck in a drought: a mental/spiritual/emotional RUT.

Since they were apathetic to depth they labeled me a nut cuz I couldn't/wouldn't conform to sick.

The more we're trauma-bonded due to increased broken families the more promiscuity, predictably.

You DESERVE success--get that through your head. You've worked, waited, prayed for and fasted.

Many independent films are clever but I found many are also horrible, callous and cruel too.

You widen the threshold levels beyond which people object and it desensitizes all of us you nut.

People are threatened the spouses wanna live separate. I mean REALLY threatened--why is that?

COMMUNIST TAKEOVER

Communist styles: We're gonna be blatantly obvious hypocrites and never apologize for it.

Made America great again/put economy back twice, brought us back to life/made a helluva sacrifice.

Lord, they're lined up at the gate and the cities are burning. Troops are everywhere and it's frightening.

Critical Race Theory propounds white guilt/inferiority. It is evil as can be that's why B*den loves it see.

AMERICA'S DAFT ERA

Mr. President Donald Trump: We are thinking of you and anxiously awaiting your next move too.

Fascism should be called corporatism as it's the merger of state and corporate power. Mussolini

Under fascism nothing is printed if unapproved by the state and the tiny group controlling corporations.

Communism: We're gonna do blatantly obvious hypocrisy and we're not gonna apologize for it too.

As a liberal my emotions/feelings ruled and there was no common sense or logic: that's a fool.

BARBARIANS LINED UP AT THE. GATE

JUST LIKE with the fall of Rome the barbarians [outsiders with different /lowerways] lined up at the gate.

Haters gotta hate--the windowbreakers at night hate Biden as much as they hate Trump, the one blamed.

You jump on the hate-Trump bandwagon like you're something, in high school tho' dumbed.

All liberals act like they're in high school. Popularity, conformity, cool, odd girl out, treacheries.

What's the cool thing to do--morals not in the stew--and adapt to the crowd: that's the liberals.

Not right or wrong, not what God wants, not what's biblically sound but whatever's goin' around.

We've reached a point where we can't be friends. No way with you condoning infanticide of the dems.

What a phony press secretary. Saying "Biden is a Catholic" like that explains it tho' his edicts are Satanic.

AMERICA'S DAFT ERA

Military turned their backs on Biden--what a humiliation! Somethings happening and God's smiling.

Your boring church potlucks are NOT a requirement for salvation, that's just you wanting attention.

It seems Mrs. Social Charm is more saved than the others, always confusing extroversion with salvation.

MULTI-LEVEL ABUSE

Like a moth to flame the trauma-bonded woman goes back into the game more dangerous each time.

Like Blanche in Streetcar she escaped to arms of boys because everyone else seemed her enemies.

They were pugnacious at my differences and for a crowd shouting diversity it sure was suspicious.

How you stayed so long is is an enigma growing but alas you're gone and I've never been so glowing.

Tho' they beat her up the prostitute went back to the same ship again and again: that's the trauma bond.

FRUSTRATION LEADS TO AGGRESSION

Held down and misjudged like that she gets aggressive and then she's really had it and that finishes it.

There are genetic mental defects then those suffering abuse from relatives until they lost it.

When they can't put up with abuse anymore they develop personality disorders they're blamed for.

The world gets smaller when you retire but used correctly the internet makes life large again sir.

AMERICA'S DAFT ERA

Her insecurities are her prevention spirit. They prevent her from fulfilling a great destiny or even to diet.

All of society's rejection energy is constantly deforming our concept of self, so pray for daily renewing.

DUMBED DOWN MILLENNIALS

It's embarrassing how immature/deluded Millennials are. Knowing nothing about gov it's all slogans/slurs.

The boys are stupid but the girls are far stupider. They cling to gov like daddy/morally in the gutter.

The girls are dumber than boys cuz they conform to anything deployed to fill that big void.

What can we do with children over 30 when grandparents are just as deluded and immoral see?

It makes you feel good to repeat yourself constantly but unfortunately it's a waste of my mental energy.

Don't presume friendship then start asking for things. I don't even know you/choose my own friends.

ONE WORD IS ALL IT TAKES

I've been so beaten up all it takes is **ONE WORD** and I'm outa your matrix cuz I'm above you hicks.

Just **ONE WORD** reveals universes of meaning, more than a library of books to those who are discerning.

Trauma is like being in a war where there's never any R & R. It can go on for decades blocking your star.

Gang-rape victims shaking and crying years later as if the event is now, right here--imagine the terror.

AMERICA'S DAFT ERA

The invasive boys are now in their fifties with no idea what they did to me—ya just have to forgive, see.

No gang-rape victim can allow you to come with all your friends [flying monkey army] to her house.

What makes man human is seeing signs symbolically and symbols significantly: that's intuition see.

The long and short of this is: you don't know what you're talking about/are making an ass of yourself.

SIGNS OF GLOBALISM

If it comes out of nowhere and suddenly it's everywhere that's the globalist agenda for sure.

Biden will now help ALL of you to turn your states red in opposition to his policies of utter death.

We gotta tie the hands of the big spenders in DC and let that be the goal of each and every proceeding.

Will we ever forget the frightening opening days of the Biden administration's extremist policies?

They don't care what you think anyway. Under the socialists' control you don't even exist ok?

Now Donald Trump can be President of the World--moving and talking without restrictions, good.

COMMIE CULTS

In this communist cult objecting to an election is grounds to have your life and business cancelled.

The double standard of punishments for conservatives made us get out/relocate to the periphery.

AMERICA'S DAFT ERA

He **DIDN'T** throw us to the wolves. He couldn't, he didn't, just be patient as military arrests all traitors.

Calling us violent, conflating patriots with violence but not caring about all the burning liberal cities.

Trump's coming back! Daddy never left us! Just hang on and trust the plan the Health Ranger said.

75 MILLION BROKENHEARTED AMERICANS

75 million Americans are brokenhearted today. This Biden inauguration is a lie cuz they stole it ok?

The Trumpster said: it's like your first love suddenly saying it's over, she never meant it to be forever.

In fact she's leaving today when you thought you'd be making your home great again together.

He's **NOT** gone. It's a temporary military operation [led by Flynn] as old gov ends and New Republic begins.

He **HAD** to get the hell out while all this was going on. Why should he put up with anything more hon'?

Under Gen. Flynn the military arrests 500,000 traitors of indictments sealed-- then we see the sex videos.

THERE'S A PLAN MAN

Don't worry, Trump did **NOT** leave us to the wolves. We'll be laughing soon as his genius plot's revealed.

Giving these people reins of power in America is beyond terrible for what they have planned man.

The Steal: They're not smart, they're not good tacticians or great strategists they're just EVIL.

AMERICA'S DAFT ERA

Free speech has never been so dangerous in United States of America as it from today 20 January.

He hasn't left us in this awful situation. Expect a blackout across nation with videos of confessions!

This seals the divide already felt in families. Now it's an unbridgeable gulf so go ahead and leave.

The pervasive/sudden fear of speaking freely will definitely strip you of creativity and make you boring.

In a minute we went from most loved president to radical communist fascists who wanna kill us.

It's gotten so bad it's a sign only Jesus can save us. When things got this trashed they called a fast.

The Insurrection Act was signed last Friday--give it a chance. The fastest thing is military arrests.

HOW DO WE LIVE NOW

How do we live in the China Biden Commie Harris kingdom when we thought we're getting great again?

Liberal deprogramming will be to get you to accept three families coming to live in your house or else.

He conflated racism with America's history then redeemed himself as its savior and moral authority.

His talk of "unity" is a worn-out banality all while he brings division by constantly stoking racism see.

The idea women bring tenderness to politics is insane--female dictators are warhawk's during reign.

Tho' enemy is more powerful than ever he's also more afraid and exposed than ever, so persevere.

AMERICA'S DAFT ERA

DC under Military explains why Trump went peacefully--they are catching everyone, checkmate.

CENCORIOUS SNIPPY CULTURE

Something happens, they get censured and we say "I told you so" but too late, it doesn't matter now.

Nationalism and the process of segmentary oppositions: external conflict breeds internal solidarity.

"We have to end this uncivil war" and then he signs the most incredibly divisive orders into law.

After suddenly turning around and backstabbing their very loyal audience, Fox News is finally done.

Before Trump, money in Washington could buy anything. But now things have changed: a true divine king!

His election is as big as 1776. If he delivers he'll be bigger than Geo Wash despite the propaganda hex.

Trump's gonna do it or die trying. Kill him, it doesn't matter--he'll work all day and night to stop our crying.

Long patient planning is the essence of world building. The real Trump was hiding in plain view I think.

BUT THE GLOBALISTS BLOCKED US

There have been tyrants and murderers who for a time seem invincible but in the end always fall.   Ghandi

Trump's driven, focused and stubborn when he sets his mind. That's our guy: not giving an inch, how refreshing!

He's focused on infrastructure cuz he's a builder--that's what he does. We're so fortunate after what was.

AMERICA'S DAFT ERA

President of the United States is pro-life. Get used to it you wicked witches creating so much strife.

I'm telling you it was all demons. Jesus healed the sick by throwing em out then it's over for them.

Jesus Christ is not dominance and submission but mercy and forgiveness. Believe in Him and you'll never die.

Royalty is not about how you're born but repentance and the reward is right-brain living and a life of giving.

Our anthem celebrates those who died for our country not grievances by brats filled with money.

Whoa: now "climate denial" is premeditated murder? Just when we think leftists can't get crazier.

Under Trump they've only arrested ten thousand pedophiles--and they say he's done nothing at all?

They just don't understand such a great mind so they attack, ridicule, lambaste and call him an ass.

Bill Maher, a very sick comic, says "trade leaders with us" cuz he loves Rocketman and hates Trump.

THEY'D RATHER HAVE OBAMA

They'd rather have Obama--perfect speech covering chicanery, theft, collusion and treachery.

So steeped in liberalized thought for 40 years when a real intellect comes along they can only fear.

The things they believe in makes them scum. But they could repent and change then we'd forgive em.

They're triggered by his speech, still under the influence of Trump Derangement Syndrome in creeps.

AMERICA'S DAFT ERA

They want us walking on eggs to avoid triggering them. Don't do this--speak up, be bold, slam em.

INTERLOCKING JEALOUSY SYSTEMS

Le Bron James is buddy with Hillary. He campaigned for her so of course he's displaying this treachery.

We love Trump, the best. We love his words unlike you picking bones in trivia, misreading what he says.

They're still freaking out in a panic. So they've resurrected the Kapernick caper to keep on hitting it.

If you're a conservative you'll be 86ed by all your liberal friends. Dis-friended, dis-owned, spat on.

It's not a Trump cult--we're not like you. We just tremendously admire, finally, a common sense view.

They are dumbed down and made mean. These traits go together in the public school scene.

Our great love for Trump: We're not blind dummies: If he starts to go sideways we'll throw him out.

They wanna kill it cold: The American resurgence movement is free market, beautiful and bold.

You know he didn't mean that S.O.B. stuff but of course you will make a big thing out of it.

Rich brats attacking our national symbols.

Just because it's legal doesn't mean you should do it.

JUST CUZ IT'S LEGAL DON'T DO IT

Standing is homage to our great heritage of freedom and for those players, prosperity for the dumb.

AMERICA'S DAFT ERA

Poor people are poor because they think poor. Dr. Ben Carson

Hollywood's failing losing half it's audience cuz we're sick of hearing about boring social justice.

Calling it "the herd" is not an insult to people but social hypnotism vs. individualism of Christians.

Liberals will come at you any way they can--banning, censuring or ostracizing from the clan.

African pastors are less sullied by the leftist bullies and speak biblical truth undaunted by the silly.

Haha Trump's having a ball: Every time he says anything the ants go crazy running around, appalled.

Trump talks, the ants scramble. HA HA HA

London: When ants get stood on they carry on as normal and wait for the next step to fall. Kate Hopkins

INFORMED DISSENT VS. PACK DISSENT

There's informed dissent and pack dissent. The latter's where we're at and it's bad. Bill O'Reilly

The left drives the narrative that USA is an evil country because they wanna change everything.

You take a family to the football game and it costs a grand. How are they gonna react to no-stands?

The NFL league does not allow pro-American demonstrations, but it's ok for player-creeps no-stands?

The Cowboys wanted to honor local police killed--not allowed. But it's ok to hate America--how fowl!

We can't have a constitution that "they" made, we gotta have a new one--that's their whole game.

AMERICA'S DAFT ERA

They don't want capitalism, electoral college or white people dictating so mobilize minorities to be angry.

MASCULINITY BAD, AMERICA-HATE GOOD

"Toxic masculinity" is what the left calls football but with America-haters they're all-ok?

It's the contagion of madness as now everyone's kneeling and they have no idea why they're doing it.

Race-hustlers on the assault with media as their calvary. Time to retreat and then win the rivalry.

America-hating athletes would prefer the Cuban, North Korean or Venezuelan national anthem.

Krazy Kapernick wears Castro or Che tee shirts. He really knows about civics doesn't he, that jerk.

Let em win then see their end. We'll play the Cuban anthem followed by rap music/halftime sex sin.

NFL players are arrested every seven days on average. But maybe it's culturally-ok to be a savage.

THUG BACKLASH

What a great thug-backlash in the NFL! Loyal fans are burning jerseys and told em to go to hell!

A trickle into heaven, a flood into hell. Kapernick a Christian until Muslim girlfriend cast her spell.

It must be terrible to be famous and make an ass of yourself. In interviews maybe best to just shut up.

Nixon won after two olympiads gave black power salute. Keep it up and we'll go more Right to boot.

AMERICA'S DAFT ERA

They see us as an evil country where white supremacists stalk innocent blacks: not true, not a fact.

Why not kneel for the 300,000 black babies aborted per year or the 2000 black-on-black murders?

Moral grandstanding, virtue signaling, emotional incontinence--until faced with the consequences.

They virtue signal, calling him a white supremacist but now their career is over, good riddance!

FEMALE THUGS IN POLITIX

"It's not about making America great again but making it white". Maxine Watters, dingbat/not too bright.

Pathetically poor thinkers destroying our country by virtue signaling over nothing: trifles, bluffing.

The left is also fascistic about diet dogma then weak minds cave into them and it's the end of ya.

Their arrogance brought such a backlash now the American resurgence is stronger than ever--hah!

WE'RE SICK OF BEING BULLIED BY CREEPS

We're sick of being bullied by you creeps. We've had it, it's stupid and spreading like terrorists.

50 percent said they'll avoid NFL now it's protested Trump, our fella

NFL'S like a black cloud now: ingrates. So much crime, arrogance, hatred of country. You're fired.

NFL used to mean Americana--no more. Globalist pawns, haters of country, traitors, whores.

Now a sudden divide--a gulf much wider than ever before. It's the final straw, that's all, and WOW

AMERICA'S DAFT ERA

Saying our president is divisive when what he says the majority agrees with.

"Women had better sex under socialism" why cuz they gotta turn to prostitution?

A major grassroots populist reallignment--a RESET. This is exhilarating and historically EPIC!

Pressure and censorship has only blown up in their face. America is coming back in grace.

Nationalism is an important global movement not just here but worldwide and how exciting I love it.

WE'RE AWAKE NOT A CULT

How do we drain the swamp? By flooding it with populists and then they'll be gone and we won.

FOX is blended, parroted BS showing one side--the establishment, Tucker/Hannity aside.

Trump is executing you with your own ignorance and arrogance and he's gonna finish the job, dunce.

Trump forced a fight and the enemy took the bait. 70% now saying this is insane and they hate it.

AMERICA HATERS ARE DOMINATING

Bunch of America haters trying to culturally dominate us using the NFL venue and we said hell with you.

FOX is milquetoast crud like CNN and it's such a disappointment when you tune in.

How to destroy a billion dollar business: inject offensive leftist politics and alienate your customer base.

Our brilliant genius president flushed em out and they took the bait bringing a backlash of hate.

AMERICA'S DAFT ERA

As in 1984, due to distractions like games and handouts the larger evils invariably escaped their notice.

Those who hated Trump the most and propounded thus will be hated and toast--what a cosmic joke!

NFL and Hollywood hijacked by social engineers to distract from larger evils/advance globalism.

Now, due to its sheer arrogance, the NFL's star power will decline just like the mainstream media.

Just cuz you have the right to do it doesn't make it right.

BLM is a highly funded anarchist racist organization leading to cop killings and from that came Kaepernick.

We don't care if you call us white supremacists the world has woken up to what you've done/it sux.

Their capitulation makes em even more weak.

Trump's gotta do what he's gonna do to protect us and our children, but of course they'll criticize him.

CHIPS ON SHOULDER GETS ATTENTION

It's cool, fun, attention getting--the more chips on your shoulders the higher status in that setting.

NFL Bull: Everyone's got a sick feeling they're in the enemy camp being preyed on by a bunch of losers.

NFL Unified hype--unified peer pressure from a bunch of followers.

If you don't accept you're bad, racist and evil they'll get you fired.

On this anti-American NFL crap: they're getting paid by big foundations but we don't care about that.

AMERICA'S DAFT ERA

They're trying to break our will by getting us to accept we're bad, racist, evil so we'll accept all this.

SELL COUNTRY OUT/IMPOVERISH NATION

Sell country out, impoverish nation, make all films Chinacentric commie-supportive, love enemy leaders.

They think hating America empowers them--ha ha wait and see friends.

We don't care about Trump's macho posturing (we love him for it) we hate Kapernicks cowardly kneeling.

Same boring talking points.
Thoughtless joiners and lemmings will go along with anything.

They want a kept president whom they can maneuver towards destruction.

People just wanted to relax and watch a football game not get beat over the head with a bunch of BS.

Your fake apologies are to no avail--we're not gonna ever forget this terrible traitorous tale.

Throwing a fit in the candy aisle: How embarrassing when we all thought the players had such style.

HAHA The NFL is losing millions if not billions between lost ads and federal subsidies and we just love it.

Everything they do is free speech until you wanna stand for the national anthem then you're up a creek.

WORTHLESS APOLOGIES

BS upon BS your apologies are worthless and we'll continue to boycott the ungrateful NFL nuisance.

The NFL black cloud/stink reflects exactly the milleneals and eve before that.
Public schools = dirty rats.

AMERICA'S DAFT ERA

The whole tiny town voted for Obama and oh man the hell I went thru as a conservative in America.

Liberals would put bombs in my mailbox cuz I wouldn't succumb to pure bull of leftist goons.

"Loving" liberals get violent: pugnacity/hitting when you refuse to go alone with it--pure bull of left.

The NFL thing is pivotal, a game-changer, the last straw, hitting other issues like football widows.

Sadistic devils that say "we are oppressed by the fascism of Christianity" remind of the same today.

They go away to school to get screwed up/it's the devil so when they come back, better fence up.

We're through taking their lip--them virtue signaling then forcing us to adapt. No more, that's that.

Hugh Hefner is iconic only because our culture is so degraded.

They didn't love Heff for his sophistication but his obscenity and open hatred of traditional morality.

ONE PORN KING DESTROYED THE FAMILY

Heffner was instrumental in destroying public support for monogamy and thus destroyed the family.

Most liberals are on medication, being mentally ill.

When perverts are put in prison liberals call it a "repressive climate".

How Heff is remembered shows the state of the culture. To the left an icon, to the right a lecher.

Playboy is pornagraphy.

AMERICA'S DAFT ERA

Put a fancy heady article in so the buyer feels an intellectual not a voyeur--standard trick of Heffner.

It is dishonest to accuse Trump of racism because he called em names--he attacks everyone the same.

Antifa justifies violence in response to oppression which is subjective so where does it end?

INSIPID VACUOUS POLITICAL OPINIONS

Insipid vacuous political opinions is what we hear from youngins.

Weiner and Heff: Horrible men, truly--ruined the family intentionally, disgusting perverts in reality.

Liberal feminist treachery/tricks: They said I never got my degree but would never check to see.

Reaction to Heff death clearly shows who they are right or left and the latter is dirty, dark and daft.

He's a poor baby in the New York Times: "Why I admire Anthony Weiner". Disgusting, over the line.

ELITES INTO THE OCCULT

Elites are into the occult: Skull and Bones, Bohemian Grove: both parties and the worst is Hillary.

They have no conscience or empathy it's just about virtue signaling while scalping our country.

Political correctness in it's rigidly organized thinking is over until you meet with Antifa the stabbers.

Walking around in a pussy hat vulva is all you'll do for the cause without ever asking God above ya.

THEY JUST LOVE THE ACTION

AMERICA'S DAFT ERA

"I don't know what Antifa's all about but I'll be there--just name when and where I really don't care".

Don't expect me to know anything man but to be part of the event--It's who I am.

Because you've overdone the racism thing you've deadened the cause and it'll soon mean nothing.

Trump's laughing: from an inconsequential statement to unbelievably ridiculous snowballing.

Your freedom of speech is important, mine isn't cuz I'm not black, brown or a victim who's kept down?

Whether it's a neck tattoo or what you chew it's all a **FAD** and it's bad--just listen to God your Dad.

If you don't know what you're talking about, don't say a thing. That includes Antifa/all politicking.

The **NFL** thing was to activate Antifa's declaration of war, 100 years after happened in Russia of course.

After this democrats will be ashamed cuz they were addicted to snide hits on Trump but lost the same.

ANTIFA HAS COLLEGES AND MEDIA

Antifa has the colleges and media--they've got it all--and aim non-lilberals to be killed/take a fall.

They're afraid of the cornucopia of the free market which will soar under Trump's tax cuts--panicked!

Crude/gross/immature/silly but a gorgeous sonorous unforgettable voice--man has two sides.

It's like anesthesia: you can't fight back you only slip into adaptation and your reality goes black.

AMERICA'S DAFT ERA

CREEPY OLD PORNOGRAPHERS

Hugh Heffner was a creepy old pornographer so why are the left celebrating him? Ben Shapiro

To see how it's all a herd, notice how strange ideas spread like wildfire--then they simmer out/expire.

NFL football turned into a social justice warrior institution has alienated the fan base who loved em.

It wasn't Michael Jackson and/obscene gestures who was King of Soul it was James Brown on a roll.

Saying they're abusing you when all they wanted was your approval but they gave up now cuza you.

You blame Donald Trump for black poverty inner cities? That's ridiculous it's all a democrat tragedy.

How could so many people be wrong? Cuz it's groupthink, social hypnotism, the herd, a swarm.

To blame all of America for the sins of a few is just nasty and silly but it's happening to me/you too.

A classic Marxist tactic is to put down a patriot as a racist.

It's a Marxist-Communist psychological operation for total destruction and Obama's behind it.

THEY WANT ANGER, VIOLENCE AND CLASH

They want anger, violence, a clash--white vs. black, make it all about that.

Hah: the race card is pulled by politicians, academics and celebrities--in fact, everybody.

Las Vegas was the worse mass shooting in American history.

AMERICA'S DAFT ERA

You can't talk logic to madness and nothing to stupid so stop trying and enjoy life free of the insipid.

We can be Nineveh not Babylon but maybe we'll get worse first.

Stop misinterpreting my Christian restraint as weakness cuz I can see right through you dingbats.

Reason she went wrong: liberal thoughts. Trying to act out some feminist role her soul never bought.

AFGHANISTAN

Our leaders are risk-averse: they fear casualties and lack spine. Jack Keane, Study of War.

It's a moralistic failure unimaginable for the people of the United States of America. Nikki Haley

The very IDEA we'd leave Americans and friends to die after serving America is beyond sad.

We know how to deal with the Taliban. Yes it's a great risk but a noble effort. Jack Keane

It's the same violent group who stone women but we can trust the Taliban, just ask Biden.

Stupid, arbitrary, politically-motivated deadlines bring ruin especially when you tell em.

Create an humanitarian crisis, arm the enemy then go back on vacation--can you imagine?

BOTCHED BY WRONG ASSUMPTIONS

It was actually botched by wrong assumptions from the liberal narrative and simplistic slogans.

Disaster: Planning only for best case scenarios while minimizing violence or seriousness of foe.

AMERICA'S DAFT ERA

America's the greatest country ever was. Not perfect but our values need to be defended fast.

The left is linked with Islam--anyone against the west--so of course Biden underestimates Taliban.

It's a global ad for resurgence of terrorism while looking down at the treacherous Americans.

If you make decisions by the calendar on the wall not conditions on the ground you're doomed.

IT'S CLASSIC GROUPTHINK

It's classic groupthink where you have a bubble who thinks one way and blocked from change.

If things aren't working and you're seen flip flopping they won't believe anything you say.

The bureaucracy runs a country everyone knows that, so watch out if they're schooled as brats.

They always underestimate our military. Said 30 years to rid ISIS, Trump did it in 18 months.

Where are you phony feminists about what's about to happen to women/girls in Afghanistan?

They have a utopian view of the world--they can't see an enemy so make horrible deals see.

If we don't remember Dude what made America great then the whole world is screwed.

Australia didn't have a second amendment so all their guns were taken. We have it tho' threatened.

A old man suffering with dementia with his finger on the trigger to wipe us out in America.

AMERICA'S DAFT ERA

The Taliban like ISIS uses fashion to evoke excitement and you can see this recruitment device.

It's a dangerous world when America's a harmless enemy/treacherous friend: the end.

Remove Americans first, then equipment, bomb all bases, bring back military. Pres. Trump

CONSTANT ERRORS OF INFERIOR MINDS

We gave our enemies 600,000 rifles, 2000 armored vehicles, 40 aircrafts and 7 new choppers.

This is what to do: Remove ALL the military and then bring em all back to get civilians maybe.

Joe Biden wants to give Taliban 500 million in foreign aid in return for winning the war.

It isn't what liberals don't know that scares me, it's what they know that isn't true. Ronald Reagan

The boots on the ground get it right but the suits in Washington are outa touch day/night.

When the world thinks America is harmless as an enemy and treacherous as a friend. B. Lewis

Our men will have to go back with no bases, no allies and fighting their own equipment.

Mass immigration is meant to disenfranchise citizens who can't be persuaded to vote left.

We are broken by the begging and cries for help from the abandoned cuz Biden said to stop.

It's the reality of war: All through history the victor takes your property and your territory.

AMERICA'S DAFT ERA

All our decisions should be conditions-based: We get all our people out THEN we go home ok.

Running on HOPE results from the politicization of the national security apparatus: no clout.

LAWLESS ELECTED LEFTISTS

Lawless elected leftists break our laws all the time and suffer no punishment for it, aye.

These are epic times. Like WW II people felt they could die any minute. What's your destiny in this?

I don't wanna know strange brutal customs I wanna be around people like me, a dwindling minority.

Biden's snarky answer: "you'll be the first to know". How callous and stubborn of the ol' geezer.

We left our people behind in a country they can't get out of. "Just get to the airport" says Biden.

It's not what you say to the Taliban that's important it's what they hear. Kayleigh McEnany

Impeach the president and fire the brass. Don't forget and sink in your swill that's all I ask.

America is the biggest supplier of arms to terror groups so who is the threat to democracy?

Imagine liberal indignation if it were Trump looking at his watch at the Dignified Transfer.

You can't bargain with terrorists alright? They only get strength, leverage and military might.

GANGS OF YOUNG MALES

AMERICA'S DAFT ERA

The problem all over the world is young males. ISIS, terrorists, rapists, militaries, gangs.

Having been attacked by a gang of young males half a life ago I pity with Afghan females.

It's an inveterate traditional gender war and they've already won it. It's dungeons or adapt.

Young males lack empathy but lotsa imagination and energy, for a victim its a catastrophe.

Gist of eldering: mining the past for gems. With lucid recall we can see what it all means.

He's a lost man acting like he's found. He's empty and dependent on likes from you, the crowd.

God restored my youth as the eagle just as He said He would in the bible and I'm relieved so.

The problem is you can't unsee that movie once you've seen it. You try but it intrudes and repeats.

AT TIMES LIKE THIS

At times like this we're to pray for our leaders, for it's a very dangerous time for every one of us.

This is such a dangerous time--unheard of. And it's gonna increase suddenly, God protect us!

Democrats are far bigger threat to freedom than the Russians but no one believes it for some reason.

Accumulation is cheap and if you don't have a place for it don't keep. Stuff stacked here/there: gee.

Stay on your own page cuz no one understands a sage.

AMERICA'S DAFT ERA

Stay on your own page and kick em offa your page--that's how you stay sane in the cruel computer age.

SUFFER THEN WRITE

I suffer, I squeeze out a nugget: I write, it's resolved for a minute. Then I suffer again darnit.

Calvinists neat as a pin (reflect divine), free-willers messy doing what they want (acting like swine).

Are their ratings rising with disasters increasing? Can't help wondering

EVIL IS A CONSUMING FIRE

Evil is like a fire consuming everything it meets. That's social hypnotism but Christians have restraints.

Packaging your life according to what they wanna hear is not gonna work, it comes off as corny sir.

Yes, its about love--but what about defending ourselves and killing the ruthless invader? No talk

Who can take so much falsehood all around? Who wants to be exposed to anti-Trumps and their jargon?

They don't know anything, that's their problem. It's all about virtue signaling not keeping em out.

Virtue signal then go fill your face.

Every country wants it's people to be un-armed.

The left said they were coming Oct. 1 and ramping up Nov. 4. They are geared up for this, no joke.

Country western: congregation of conservatives and gun owners--can you see the bigger picture?

AMERICA'S DAFT ERA

Country folk are "bitter clingers" to the left. They hate God-and-gunners who heed what God says.

They're always exploiting death and tragedy to take away our gun rights.

They want to impose large government on America (statist) so want to take away our guns, it's obvious.

THE DISARMED ARE EASILY MANIPULATED

If disarmed we're easily manipulated.

Gun culture has driven down crime 60% since 1992. Gun-free cities have the highest crime rate too.

If it'd been a hiphop concert woulda had severe leftist backlash but bitter clingers deserved it?

Our country is divided between big and small government, not like in the sixties martini vs potheads.

Fems won't protest brutal oppression of Islamic women and that reveals how good they have it here.

They aren't just bashing Trump they're frothing--it's ongoing, gearing up for violent killing.

UNEARNED MORAL. SUPERIORITY

Left does nothing for the world but there is an unearned moral superiority like they have the pearl.

I don't care how much corruption is found in churches, it's all about savior Jesus Christ thru the ages.

Dems want good honest people to be defenseless in America. NRA isn't the problem it was Obama.

NRA is all about gun safety, Hollywood's all about gun violence but then these hypocrites blame us!

AMERICA'S DAFT ERA

Law-abiding people aren't the ones causing problems and should have the right to self-defense, amen.

The more lonely now the more flooded with popularity later after crossing the great divide (Ender).

Your pursuit should be self, that's style. That will lead others, not empty altruism but mad as hell.

Hypocrites want only liberal body guards to have guns, the rest of us can just pray for help or run.

Confront rich liberals: But your body guard has guns so why would you repeal the 2nd amendment?

THE NRA ARE NICE RATIONAL MEN

The NRA are such nice, rational men. Liberals have em all wrong but then they have an agenda.

NRA aren't liberal freaks sexualizing children and the like. They are good men: gun safety/doing right.

TV ads portray the blacks as thin and chic, the whites as corny, ridiculous, disheveled, weak.

TV ads portraying whites as evil and blacks as good are creating a race war that's misunderstood.

Michelle Obama hates how "the whites are here/non-whites there"--she wants diversity everywhere.

Memes he sends out are "essentially true" but a little odd yet his following has exploded and broad.

TV ads creating the race war by portraying white men as mean stupid devils: users, abusers, evil.

BARBARIANS IN OFFICE

AMERICA'S DAFT ERA

Democrats are the most barbaric horrible people to vote for late term abortion even up to birth: EVIL.

Hillary wants to kill babies up to age 2 and academics agree--we've gotten too used to these creeps.

The democrats are so evil by the things they believe in people--like killing babies after they are viable.

Democrats used to be the center but now they've gone full force into satanism, communism, murder.

They'll do anything to divide us and take our guns. Even mass murder colluding with Antifa/Islam.

Wake-up people, don't you see what they're doing? It's beyond the pale, sickening, unbelievable.

ANYTHING TO RETRIEVE POWER--*ANYTHING*

They'll do anything to retrieve money and power--anything. Think of the implications of that: think.

They take the guns when we need em the most: After disasters or false flags creating chaos.

Democrats are so left they've gone daft. Murder, satanic rituals, mass death.

Anyone impugning AMA or science gets ridiculed to the face. Old dogmas are a god/can't be defaced.

Can you say democrats are your friends? They have no friends/can't be a friend--just follow trends.

PEOPLE ARE SPLIT AND BLIND

People are split and in denial. The daily fast brings out their spirit, they face reality and become whole.

Gunman tied to Antifa, unlicensed weapons, shoots country music fans: gun laws NA, it's terrorism.

AMERICA'S DAFT ERA

Democrats are the biggest virtue signalers--they're defined by it. Compare that to what they do: think of it.

We'll just call it the Country Music Shooting from now on--rich liberals on coasts hate freedom songs.

Democrats: "country music shooting was God's message to republicans on gun control"--fools!

They hate bitter clingers loving life on the land. They want us defenseless and cooped up like hens.

They'll do anything--anything--to get that power back even a mass shooting.

SCIENCE EVOLVES LIKE ALL HERDS DO

Science evolves and also devolves so what he's saying is absolutely true taking a longitudinal view.

The less knowledgeable about firearms the more enthusiastic liberals are about controlling them.

"Still no motives" but he converted last month to ISIS. Blind as bats or just more refusal to see this?

The metal rockers easily convert to christianity after being hurt by the evil satanic influence thereby.

Even Christian music uses heavy metal--screeches from hell!

Socially hypnotized to like it, like other things. Doubt they'd wanna hear it if left to their own instincts.

Bang, bang, bang, screetch screetch screetch: That's our civilized music as we go under siege.

ANTI-TATTOO IS TABOO

You can't criticize their music or tattoos, let alone their sexual immorality-- that is all taboo.

AMERICA'S DAFT ERA

Who do you think you're dealing with, some idiot? I'm trying to draw you out so they'll all see it.

Dems don't wanna help people--it's all about them not you.

Start here, now: release old systems keeping you down--there's bad karma to (SS) Stockholm Syndrome.

It was such good practice all the suffering you did over them. Hah: And now you're ready for anything.

What are you gonna do, wish em all dead? No, just get ready for your success--go on ahead instead.

The reward for repentance from old systems keeping you down is mass attractions to your genius.

They're not the ones running the country and they can see their ways falling apart/panicking.

GUN OWNERS CALLED "TERRORISTS"

The liberal gist: All of us must give up our rights, the NRA is guilty and the gun owners are terrorists.

Arguing with idiots is teaching you apologetics.

You allowed yourself to see smut cuz you're a free willer: do what thou wilt, no restraints, a mutt.

Women responded with "playgirl" and having affairs--it was retaliatory but it debased em, no victory

Free speech is the basis of happy freedom or tyrants/groups ride roughshod over everyone else.

Don't say all youth eras were crazy too--we didn't do these destructive things and call it cool.

I was right on the cusp. Baby boomers had hobbies, projects--weren't sexualized as kids.

AMERICA'S DAFT ERA

Soros owns our education!. He's trying to demoralize us, sexualize our kids, bring us down.

No matter what they did it may be unintentional–liberalism's so entrenched it's just natural.

APOLOGETIC ARGUMENTATION

Even in the churches women are infected with feminism, you see it in how they treat husbands.

Bitter clingers: We cling to old paths which are logical, reasonable and commonsensical.

Michelle Obama wants us to live in dark/divisive world where race is more important than who we are.

God's words ask that you take a long view: Tho' they flourish now soon they'll be cut down (whew).

If a woman tries to fight a man she's gonna lose big time in all ways--there are better ways, high pay.

SCHOOLED TO THINK AMERICA'S BAD

Schooled to think America's so bad, she deserves everything she gets and libs think like that, in fact.

Left on Jails: People who've committed crimes with guns let out, and those who own a gun throw in.

It wasn't a long rambling discursive debate I was just teaching apologetics to those who hate.

We don't need heartless monsters as doctors especially those hooked to big pharma to drug ya.

Like a drunk neighbor in your yard, Hillary wondered onto another show to crap on the president.

AMERICA'S DAFT ERA

She's like a dumped EX who keeps writing long letters to his parents about how their son who screwed up.

There was a world before identity politics hogwash but now the Overton window has moved, hah

We're bigger than them, they're just a small group that won't go away.

Liberal group mind forms as they cast out dissidents. The genius misfit must say screw you to it.

Hypocrisies: The more liberal the company the more hellish their facilities, like slave factories.

"History doesn't matter cuz we have progress now: we don't need it cuz we're better/in the know."

WE'RE LIBERAL = INTELLECTUAL

We're liberal, we're intellectual--worship us!

Trudeau, Canada's pervert leader, has legalized bestiality. It's so exploitive of animals--what a tragedy.

NFL: You are not America's sport you're a globalist Hollywood filth production and it's a plan.

See every debate/argument as apologetic practice--it buffers your quick-to-shoot reactions.

Liberal louse wants to block my right to defend myself from murderous trash breaking in my house.

NFL is not American but globalist: anti-gun/anti-family trash.

Whiny opinion pieces on how to better support pedophiles. Left sees em as misunderstood minority.

Feminists against "groping of women" ignore mass rapes by Muslims.

AMERICA'S DAFT ERA

How dare you say our boys on campuses wanna rape you. They don't want anything to do with you!

Meryl Streep is a demonic creature who led a standing ovation to a child rapist.

Men seem nice and overly-apologetic now, and women are angry somehow reflected in frowns.

Why are you complaining about men in the west? They aren't groping you, it's all in your heads.

Americans don't have armed guards/live in gated communities yet we're lectured by Hollywood crazies.

OBAMA CUT THE MILITARY

"Peace will prevail by cutting our military". Obama

Just stop virtue signaling about "groping women" while ignoring massive gang rapes by Muslims.

It's become a big thing in the liberal gay community to get it and spread it-- and now California's OKd it?

Having been told it's ok--even superior--they go full force into sin and never question it (no God fear).

Hollywood, the NFL and elites in both parties are collapsing. Rats are leaving all ships, disavowing.

Liberals are in a war against white Christians. They wanna bring non-whites in and other religions.

THEY'RE DOWN ON WHITE

They're down on white men for "groping" but ignore Muslim raping: want open borders--let em all in.

Majority of Americans are white, majority of those are Christians so to take down America, target em.

AMERICA'S DAFT ERA

Since Trump they've stepped up the anti-white war calling us neo-Nazis, fascists, white supremacists.

It is part of the left's agenda to disarm us so we cannot resist the oppression they have planned.

First thing dictators do is disarm the populace so they can't resist tyranny.

The details of Roman Polanski's crime highlight Hollywood's problematic stand against Trump.

Left: gays, abortion, no borders/guns, amnesty, socialism, centralized gov, greenism, agenda 21.

Dirty filthy nasty Hollywood confirms child rape but hates Trump? Gays are switching and waking up.

Pedophilia normalized by mainstream news, NY Times and Salon. Hollywood too--babylon's fallen.

9 out of ten murders of blacks are done by blacks, in gun-free zones like Chicago: that's a fact.

ONCE YOU SEE THE ENEMY

Once you see the enemy for what they truly are, they become what they truly are. John Bound

You anti-American Hollywood filth, you narcissistic NFL evil scum, you bread and circus whorehouse.

Daddy wears a jersey with another man's number, his kids play videos, smoke crack or get drunker.

Arrested development, exercise of idiocy--it's a wonderful thing seeing this happen to the enemy.

Fired the pervert, rats leaving the sinking ship, Meryl praises child rapist, backlash: victory in Christ!

AMERICA'S DAFT ERA

Hollywood scum: devil worship/pedophilia isn't enough for em, now they wanna mess over America.

They wanna hurt middle America--not the liberal coasts (terrible) but down home decent clingers.

Leftists wanna sow discord between the races, sexes and generations: that's what they do.

Angry if you don't like what they like/do what they do. It's really weird: dumbed down human zoo.

Most popular actress Meryl Streep applauds child rapist! This has gone too far but will the left resist?

HOLLYWOOD CONTROLLED BY CHICOMS

Hollywood controls California/Sacramento: "This disease is not a stigma" so they're gonna give it to ya.

People will get HIV through unmarked donated blood,ok? It's nothing less than murder by the state.

Watch for HIV to explode in California, with sex diseases off the charts. Imagine the broken hearts.

California not only became debauched, now it's destroying itself: how sin evolves in the good book.

Is it ok to give em hepatitis and not tell em?

LATE LIBERAL SHOVE DOWNS

Spreading HIV is serial murder, okayed by the state--following a fad in gay communities of "Aids-rape".

Hillary loved to represent monsters, pedophiles and serial killers--bet you didn't now that about her.

What they are: murderers. How: pass a law you can give HIV-blood to naive/innocent bystanders.

AMERICA'S DAFT ERA

They teach 5 year olds masturbation (pedophile training) and sexualize children but that's "tolerance".

Bug-chasing (AIDS-giving) is "chic" and "misunderstood" but it's pure lunacy with hearts of wood.

Hill and Bill passed tainted blood too--diseased, passed off on Canadians, 100,000 didn't pull through.

California says it's ok to spread lethal disease, then they spin it like there's some morality to it--see?

The legalization of bug chasing in liberal gay California: "This will get rid of the stigma"--whoa!

Californian's dumb lemmings following them down a rat hole with a liberal utopia the promised end.

L.A. Times glowing: How great, you can give blood now without telling em--how loving and enchanting!

THEY LOVE THE DEVIANCE OF HURTING INNOCENCE

They enjoy the deviance of bringing others down with em. Like crabs in a bucket that's liberal scum.

Pedophiles, scum, fiends: That's who wants your guns, your kids and for you to take vaccines.

If you say how great America is you'll be deleted, but knife-wielding madmen are well-treated.

Anything of patriotic value is deleted from youtube. Tho' it's a complement it may happen here too.

Narcissistic, crazy and like Hillary won't go away--never giving up/getting more bizarre each day.

Golden Girls: Dirty, sad comedy with a smiley--did these ol' girls start the revolution into tragedy?

AMERICA'S DAFT ERA

MINING DOWNWARD FOR HELL

The left is always mining downward searching for the hell they want--that's cuz their sin is never enough.

Lady Gaga says she's a devil worshipper. Listen, know em, understand the implications, boycott em.

They support lawlessness/painting on a black canvas.

They shut down anyone with common sense and decency.

Wanna destroy the country, suppressing everything that is waking people up: they are the enemy.

To the left "polarizing views" means anything they don't agree with.

Hollywood is now a political tool to bludgeon people into compliance, not to make good movies for us.

Now that he's been fired, NOW they take the moral highroad. So typical of the treacherous liberals.

Liberals think they are morally superior. Can you imagine that with all the things they believe in--weird.

They were "completely unaware" of the horrifying claims. Oh come on, you knew it all along dames.

LIBERALS SWITCH WITH THE WINDS

Liberals switch sides with the winds. No loyalty or stability, it's all about what works with fiends.

Hollywood people have a fundamental inability to identify immorality or even downright evil.

It's shocking, it stinks. Glittering emptiness of Hollywood finks hiding, cowering or relying on shrinks.

AMERICA'S DAFT ERA

Atheists drove God out but didn't give man a way to identify evil without understanding God or the devil.

EVIL STINKS

Evil stinks, it's dark, it hurts, it's scary and wretched yet the godless atheist can't see this I'll betcha.

Perhaps the worst thing about your crazy people is their inability/lack of desire to identity evil.

Capacity to identify evil thru body language, silences, vocal tones, pauses, sinister disappearances.

The driving out of God without the capacity to identify evil is the great tragedy of the 21st century.

Men are afraid of female emotions cuz they've been made to squelch theirs. Understanding: fresh air.

Man's higher mind of acute intelligence makes em stark raving mad if starting from wrong premise.

The best saints were the worst sinners because they saw the result of evil and enjoy being winners.

ACTRESS ADORES A CHILD RAPIST

WITCH: Meryl Streep can't distinguish freaks and pigs--she loves, adores and adulates a child rapist.

There's not a shred of true passion in their moral outrage--it's perfunctory just for applause on stage.

The creepy Hollywood scum don't care about a thing--they've known about pizzagate, ya think?

People adapt to their mate, but if he's crazy there's a contagion of madness (very bad fate).

AMERICA'S DAFT ERA

Disgusting rich and all their debaucheries, thinking money will protect them--
we'll just have to see.

MOORE MORAL CONSCIENCE

Michael Moore--moral conscience of America--said Harvey Weinstein's the
best guy ever, no kidding ya.

Michael Moore's whole thing: his capacity to detect evil corruption (aren't we
sick of these pigs?)

Michael Moore claims the capacity to detect immorality and corruption--
enough of fat pig anti-guns.

The liberals make decisions on what they want to see (utopia) rather than what
exists, true reality.

Since all men are sinners, mistakes are always made. But that's no reason to
hate America, just PRAY.

Utopian liberals can see what is distant (ideas) but not what's right in front of
them (like North Korea).

Jimmy Kimble (the back of the classroom idiot conscience of America) will
take him on now he's disarmed.

Now that he's fired and out of favor: "he's terrible, unconscionable , horrible"

We're so sick and tired of the NFL and Hollywood stars. Morally out to lunch,
not cool but squares.

We gotta show em money has no power with us: God and morality comes first
and they're filth, pus.

THE GODLY ARE OSTRACIZED

Any godly America-loving actor is fired/not hired. He is banned, censured,
ridiculed, not admired.

They lectured us on what is good, kind, moral and what is bad, mean and sinful
in this giant swindle.

AMERICA'S DAFT ERA

They are absolute filth in their glittering weddings and dire warnings--it's all been a sham, darlings.

CHI-COM OWNED

They have incessantly lectured us on right and wrong while covering up these stinking corruptions.

Ban Meryl Streep/put her in the trash heap. Her stinking love of a child rapist is like she did it--freak!

If you make decisions on what you WANT vs. what IS, good luck: being outa grace you'll fall into a pit.

JOB OF OLDER WOMEN

Older women should school the youth on morality, not like Meryl Streep be a disgusting dirty old lady.

Now we'll see ol' Meryl backtrack her comments. But due to the internet she'll never get out of it!

Meryl Streep is the most disgusting old lady there ever was--can't imagine anyone dirtier for applause.

Hollywood scum/Hillary sees half of America as deplorables tho' we're decent/see children as adorable.

They can see--so clear--who is bad and immoral yet they take money from this grungy guy from hell.

Obama knew about his perversions but sent his daughter to intern under him: can't see corruption.

"Sexism, misogyny, Islamophobia, homophobia" yet they're all-ok with child rape and devilish perversion.

They take the moral highroad--after the things they do/did, the perverts they loved, the smut!

AMERICA'S DAFT ERA

Meryl Streep glowed with self-congratulatory love as she led the standing ovation for that slug.

SEARED CONSCIENCES GET USED TO SIN

It's not that everyone's a pervert but thru social hypnotism we're infested, flooded, we get used to it.

How terrible this is, truly: undermining the left's claim that THEY have a superior sense of morality.

Michael Jackson's masturbatory mimicries on stage were horrible but James Brown was adorable.

Human degeneration: After James Brown it got really dirty and they loved MJ's antics: Lord have mercy.

How gross, how vile! Yet beloved by Hollywood stars who we follow/make us smile, set our styles!

Hollywood created Miley Cyrus--beyond debauched, worst-ever porn, lowest hell ever watched.

Hollywood's owned by China who wanna overcome us and how do they do this: make us moral messes.

Hollywood vultures and lechers: evil creatures who lecture us.

GLOBAL WARMING: THEY'RE ONE OF EM

Rule of thumb: Whenever one talks of global warming you know they're one of em/ ignore scum.

Stars make a mint from likability--what happens when we find they covered for this gross hillbilly?

Money and power doesn't have to corrupt absolutely.

Liberals hate conservatives because you see, libs have such a strong moral foundation of decency.

AMERICA'S DAFT ERA

They hate conservatives but praise Weinstein more than God. Wow--let this reveal the damned/flawed.

TELL ALL: Let them off their nondisclosure agreements and truly drain the swamp--let it all out!

NOW'S YOUR CHANCE TO RISE

Now's your chance to take the crown. If you're not a leftist make documentaries about em/put em down.

Hold these creeps to their own standards, don't let this be old news and let us return to decency/manners.

They can't debate so they swear.

Censured for putting down Hollywood scum.

Obama/Clinton allowed this perverted behavior. Weinstein lined pockets to keep mouths shut forever.

Democrat-Hollywood link is solid and tight so this brings down the massive edifice we've had to fight.

Hillary has shown she's complicit with powerful white men--the very men she claims to fight, amen.

Disproportionately? What about the white people killed by police--you don't ever mention that I see.

Donna Koran designs sexy teen clothes but now says don't wear em cuz it triggers men, you know.

Leftists blaming victims cuz they're wearing skirts--hypocrisy is growing in the Hollywood curse.

HYPOCRASY HOLLYWOOD

Leftists blame victims (for their dress, hating the west) while loving Islam for it's power over women.

AMERICA'S DAFT ERA

Hollywood men are silent over Weinstein. Real tough guys, wimps--opposites of real men/John Wayne.

So morally righteous about their pet projects, they disappear now to object--can you believe that?

Those most vehemently indignant are the ones who are silent--all buddies of Harvey the aberrant.

Hanging out with billionaires on giant yachts while lecturing us on our energy use: lies we bought.

Five days it took for stars/late night hosts to mention it. Why do you think that is? They're morally unfit.

HOLLYWOOD HEX

Hollywood hex: We'll hear about the pedophilia next and they can feel it breathing down their necks.

They thought they could bully us in our deep sleep induced by these creeps but God had other ideas.

Republicans are just as sick as democrats so lets call it conservatives vs. left-of-center/commie rats.

Even legal immigrants want Trump--they don't wanna throw cash in this dark hole of government.

Immigrants are no good if they're without our values. We must define the bad vs. good virtues.

ONLY CONCERN IS MINORITY DEATHS

More whites are killed by police but it's minority deaths that cause outrage in this liberal age.

Liberal government turned on the people and the unborn. It hated good and exalted evil like porn.

AMERICA'S DAFT ERA

You didn't know Nazis could be women discussing abortion like it's nothing--
they are vermin.

Don't waste time with FOX. The constant mixture with liberals (the good with
the bad) really sux.

TRUMP HATE IS BAROMETER

Let Trump-hate be your barometer of patriots wanting borders vs. liberals who
buy votes/cut corners.

Feel better since I dropped FOX. It's too social with it's jocularity, liberalism
and mixed talks.

The new world encourages quick hookups cuz they know immorality destroys-
-just look it up.

Liberal logic is illogic and it's tragic the poor decisions made from la-la land
like evil magic.

We've got to see the problem is liberalism--it's a 12-plan program all evil as
can be, amen?

She lied, period. They say it's a war on women-but it's all due to lost morals
and culture degradation.

Evil in office may have seemed smart but not as smart as Trump so take heart,
pray to God and look up.

As much a I love him I have no more time for Trump. It's now me and my work
which is to debunk.

When democrats rule what happens: crowds, crime and clutter—decay--and
never making it better.

ALL POINTS OF LIBERALISM ARE EVIL

The 12 points of liberalism are evil but social hypnotism applauds these very
things in people.

AMERICA'S DAFT ERA

First they called it Global Warming but when it got cold they switched to "climate change"--bingo.

Stevie Wonder's wrong but the blind can't research the science to see global warming's a fraud.

Obama only talked of climate change not fighting ISIS. He wanted to ruin coal mines and create crisis.

Because tyranny always follows debauchery, watch out--too many choices make a lush and louse.

HALF-TRUTHS AND BLURRED LINES

After an hour listening to Fox I realized I hadn't heard a word: half-truths and lines that are blurred.

He erased the southern border and pays to bring illegals in. And he cares about security? No, it's all spin.

Their job: to pacify, create racial division and divide while screwing us over as our life's destiny dies.

Their goal: Destabilize your central nervous system's revulsion of evil, they know you'll soon accept it all.

The white man is being pushed in the mud, all the while sayin' we want blood/are duds.

The more corrupt the state the more it legislates: Thousands more rules daily put us in dire straights.

Everything they say is inverted reality: Good is bad, bad is good, slavery is freedom--understood?

What happened to all America's brilliant innovation? It's been relegated to man's sex transformation.

CYCLES OF MANKIND

Mankind's Cycles: Things get so bad that suddenly they turn around and on all

AMERICA'S DAFT ERA

issues, revolution.

You didn't know about militarization of police? It's the opposite to their true job of "keeping the peace".

DESIRE FOR LIBERTY IS SEXY

There's nothing more sexy than desire for liberty: It's re-emerging as the way to stay high and pretty.

Homosexuals die at 42. That's the median age not accounting for AIDs, too--is the deathstyle good for you?

Cops shoot dogs (even in cages) let alone people in rages. Pray for divine reversal for our friends/charges.

The left is vacuous, empty. Though it all seems so light, glowing and friendly when it's tyranny they get petty.

56 million babies aborted and they could care less (don't even seem to know) as evil is totally supported.

Liberal thinking is the default setting from any school or university and thus most are debased and petty.

The feds are the ones who set this up, and they're not the saviors though they'll play that role while they snub.

Globalism is the opposite to local politics. It's distant, cold, obdurate while the local is kind and gentle though hicks.

Don't get sidetracked--stay on the point: It's globalism that accounts for all which disappoints.

We are losing our refinement from (centuries of genius and the Renaissance) and now we feel guilty for it?

It's a barbaric invasion just like Rome. We have different histories--like our Renaissance of old.

FIFTY YEARS OF LIBERAL MINDSET

AMERICA'S DAFT ERA

Fifty years of liberal mindset as taught in the schools and the result is what you see--catastrophe!

Hillary's all against the word "anchor babies" but it's ALL- okay to abort them, more liberal hypocrisy.

They call themselves "progressives" as if advanced--when it's back to the stone age, debauched.

We're sick of the nation ripped apart, liberalized and turned into a communist banana republic.

FEMINIST CALLOUS APATHY

There's industrial rape of women and girls going on yet feminists say nothing against Islam.

Progressives, Islamists, Nazis, communists: Understand what freedom is vs. nihilist destructionists.

Greatness of Islam? Carly must define her words here. Christianity is mercy not the bloodthirsty.

60% of America is older white--MTV says they're the problem so blacks are told to go beat em.

Race-baiting only works with dumbed down people but it works and it means violence and evil.

Since the sixties it's been the liberal mindset and Obama rode that wave--so cool, all the rave.

Women without solid foundation in the Lord are swept up with foolish fallacies they should abhor.

They're pushing race wars to a dumbed down public: Our "white privilege" gives us that guilt.

We live in a giant brainwashing cult: high-priests of ignorance, dangerous as they self-exult.

AMERICA'S DAFT ERA

Newspeak, doublethink, reduction of language. That's how it's done--telling us what to say garbage.

HEALTHYMINDEDNESS

It was a Fatal Mental Illness and you wanna blame me you hicks but I overcame it, that's the gist.

Bulimics: You had a Fatal Mental Illness that was genetic yet you felt guilty as shit and ashamed for it.

I choked in my sleep for the last time. I never, ever, ever ate past breakfast again like it's a crime.

We like being together but we like being alone better so that's the marriage of two saints I wager.

When I've had enough sugar I'm completely full/satisfied. When glycogen stores deplete hunger's high.

As a trauma-bonded child the kinda loving you need as an adult can only be given by you tho' a nut.

I don't like getting hungry and I've discovered sugar satiates perfectly until it goes on empty.

Salads, bread and butter but sometimes shrimp, tacos and I also love garlic mashed potatoes.

I had a beautiful father. If bread and butter was perfect for him it's perfect for me his daughter.

Elvis Presley the most handsome man in the world lived on peanut butter and jelly sandwiches.

WHAT WROTE THESE BOOKS

What wrote these books was being misjudged and unable to explain it until it finally exploded/this is it.

AMERICA'S DAFT ERA

I don't care about the money I just wanna be read. How else does a writer live after they're dead?

A video is too imperfect. A sentence or two I can make perfect but a video? Too many possibles.

I know what people are like when you're down and that's why I'm cool as a cucumber around em.

THE LAST IS YOUR APEX

Having the courage of your convictions—that's the necessary boldness of the Limited Election.

I think 99 times and find nothing. I stop thinking in silence and the truth comes to me. Albert Einstein.

In looking back chalk it ALL up to an evil spirit in you--don't bog down in details it was all the devil.

What is moral insanity? You feel you're on a train with no controls and you hate it all anyway.

Salvador Dali's early shyness masked a craving for attention growing alongside his talent.

Art may have been his passion but attention was his life blood. Biographer of Salvador Dali

God is not a communist nor is he even democratic. My vote means more than a seared lunatic.

KELLOCKIALISMS FALL 2021

Consensus shields idiots from accountability. That's the herd against you--a group and angry.

The godly man considers his animals. That's one way you can tell who's saved or going to hell.

AMERICA'S DAFT ERA

After having solitude you see vividly how chummy society can be, yuk three times, be free.

The last brick in the building is as important as the first. Handle completion like a crate of eggs.

When you're too weak to compete--old and grey/all you wanna do is sleep--God appears see.

See this: the most persecuted group in America are conservatives on college campuses.

The end is best--it's your crest see. The temporal lobes burst open to panoramic perception: eternity.

Since the last phase is the best, extend thirty years to 100 and spend it as a wise old happy family seer.

The weekend is here, a chance to party and celebrate whirlwind world success and nothing less.

KAREN KELLOCK

100 KAREN KELLOCK BOOKS

AFFINITY OR MISERY
AGELESS CORNUCOPIA
AMERICA AWAKE!
AMERICA'S DAFT ERA
ARTS OF PALEO FASTING
AUTOPHAGY ON CHEATERS
BACKSTABBING NEUROTICS
BETRAYAL TRAUMA
BOOMERS AND BROKENNESS
BOOT ON NECK
CHAMPION GUIDES
COMMIE NUTHOUSE
COMMIES
COMMUNIST SPIRIT
CONTAGION OF MADNESS
CONTAGIOUS MADNESS
CULTURE CLASH BASHED
DAFT LEFT
DAILY FASTARIAN
DAM RATS
DIVERSITY IS CRUELTY
E-RACE WHITE
EVIL FREAKS (Beyond Gross)
THE END OR A BEND?
FEMALE BULLIES AND FEMI-NAZIS
FEMALE CARNALITY
FEMALE DUMB DOWN
FEMALE POWER DRIVE
FEMINISM AND RUIN 1 & 2
FIX FOR MISFITS
FOOLS & TRAMPS
FREEDOM SPEAKING
FRENEMY ENABLER
FRENEMY LIAR
FRENEMY THIEF
FRENEMY TRAITOR
TRENEMY TYRANT
GENIUS IS HELD DOWN
GLOBALISLAM
GOD USES THE FLAWED
HAZE OF THE LATTER DAYS

KAREN KELLOCK PH.D.

M.S. Political Science, San Diego State. Ph.D. in Psychology, University of California Irvine. Postdoctoral: UCI School of Medicine, Dept. of Psychiatry [NIMH Grants]. Developed the Debris Theory of Disease, a theory of system pathology in 120 books and 22 textbooks for the general public. The theory has a general formula: All disease is obstruction, all recovery is elimination, all success is attraction. The three obstructions are people, habit and food. Remove obstruction and snap to your goals, waiting in the wings.